I0214319

BOSSY IS AS BOSSY DOES

THE 5 KEYS THAT OPEN DOORS

Bossy Is As Bossy Does: The 5 Keys That Open Doors

© 2016 COPYRIGHT All rights reserved. The author retains all copyrights in any text, graphic images, and photos in this book. No part of this publication may be reproduced or transmitted in any form or by any means, electronic or mechanical, including photocopying, recording, or any information storage and retrieval system, without permission in writing from the author.

This book may be published for educational, business, or sale promotional use. For information, please contact the Special Markets Division. Send an email to BossyIsAsBossyDoes@gmail.com with your request.

ISBN: 978-0-692-82345-3

Printed in the United States of America

Published by Able Publishing

Designed by Brooklyn Carter

Editor: Dr. John Lawrence Bussell

Foreword

It takes a boss to recognize a boss, and in *Bossy Is As Bossy Does*, Tara Seals delivers as expected. Her background, vast experience and 'cut to the chase' approach has produced motivating and thought-provoking nuggets in this book that will not only help you to become greater inside and out, but also prepare you to lead others to do the same.

The word "bossy" may come off a little abrasive to some but Tara cleverly explains that it's all about taking care of yourself, those you love, and by all means taking care of business. From the importance of asking for help, to admitting when you're wrong, she shares a total of five essential keys that everyone should use to unlock the authentic doors of the unlimited.

My favorite key is "To Thyself Be True". In my own life I've used this key to turn my ideas, thoughts and originality into a global brand, affording me the opportunity to inspire nations as well as befriend some of the world's most influential and wealthiest people.

There are doors in our lifetime that can only be opened with the assistance of someone before you. Tara places the keys on the front porch under the doormat, and they'll be waiting for you when you arrive.

Germaine Moody

Best-selling Author of "50 Seeds of Greatness"

Dedication

This book is dedicated to my late granny and grandpa, Ida Mae and Ellis T. Jones. I would never be able to put words together to explain how much I love and miss you guys. All my love.

Acknowledgements

First and foremost, I would like to thank God for His grace and mercy. Without HIM, I am nothing. I am beyond blessed with a supportive, praying Mama who always encourages me to do MY very best. Words can't express my gratitude to my amazing husband who has been there EVERY step of the way. I am blessed with a beautiful soul mate indeed.

Lastly, I would like to thank my clients, family, friends, business associates and partners, mentors, and my team for supporting my dreams. Thank you for your love, acts of kindness, words of encouragement, and infinite support. You are truly appreciated! Muah!

Table of Contents

By Definition

"**B**ossy is as bossy does" means EXACTLY what it says. Being bossy consists of you being the boss of yourself and making decisions based on what you need to do to meet and surpass your own personal goals. Being in control of yourself and destiny, focusing on yourself and not others, allows you to stay in your lane, recognize your personal strengths/weaknesses, and keep the main thing the main thing. Your ONLY focus is to remain focused.

When you are bossy, you do what you have to do to make things happen, no matter what, no excuses. "Excuses are tools of incompetence that build monuments of nothingness..." You know the rest. You are wasting your time making excuses, as there are NONE. They don't exist in the land of Bossy, or anywhere else for that matter. Instead, find solutions. It's all about how you "look" at the "problem."

Don't allow what it seems like at any given moment to fool you to believe that's how it will be forever, good or bad. It's not reality, and honestly, it probably never will be. Life has amazing humor, so never get comfortable. Always be ready for whatever, because it's coming. So decide the best way to approach life, even during the quirky moments, and *always* be bossy in doing so.

Once your focal point becomes how to truly be the best version of YOU, you will have the innate ability to be your FULL self...thus becoming fulfilled. *Be* bossy or *become* bossy, my friends.

Introduction

I was born on a Friday night, the firstborn child to wedded parents and my grandparents' first grandchild. Love was deeply rooted in my humble beginnings. My grandpa was a plant worker for 39 years at the same company, yet he knew the power of leaving a legacy and the way to get money as his own boss. He led by example and owned several homes and acres of land. He was an entrepreneur for over 30 years and was bossy in EVERY sense of the word...and I admired my super hero.

One day, my father decided to leave his family, my mama (his wife), my brother (age 1), and me (age 5). I questioned my grandfather about how a "man" could leave his family.

My grandpa was a man of very few words.

"Are you hungry?" he asked me.

"No, sir," I slowly replied, trying to see where he was going with this.

"Do you have everything you need and want?" he asked.

"Yes, sir."

"Okay, then."

And with that, he was done with the whole matter. In so many words, my grandpa was telling me everything would be okay, and despite the situation, he would make sure that I was good...ALWAYS. And he did just that. Integrity was everything to him. He was the epitome of a family man, moved in silence, and always handled his business. His word was bond and he was well respected among his family, friends, church, and business community.

It's funny how life works because, as a little girl, my life was shattered to tiny pieces when my father left. But God is always in control…HE runs all this, please believe! Watching my grandpa write checks at his dining room table for his kids to attend college made me work extra hard so my mama didn't have that extra stress. I worked extremely hard in school and received a full scholarship, taking the weight off my family.

I'll never forget my grandpa and granny telling me during my eleventh grade year, that if I got a full scholarship, they would buy me a new car for graduation. My 1985 sky blue Toyota Corolla, gifted to me by my mom, with the cassette player and sunroof was greatly appreciated in tenth grade back then. But a new car for college? Even sweeter!

I called them after receiving my scholarship letter in the mail. It was for a full ride to the college of my choice, The University of Memphis! Between sobs, I told my grandparents my great news and they were overjoyed! My mama was standing right next to me screaming, "Praise the Lord!" Always a man of his word, Grandpa said, "When you come in two weeks, you will get your car."

When we pulled up to the beautiful corner lot ranch-style brick home with dark red shutters that my grandpa worked so hard for, there sat an unknown car, tags and all. My grandpa and granny met us in the driveway, gave me the biggest hug ever and presented me with the keys to my new car! He'd already taught me how to change my oil and tires when I was thirteen years old. Together we did a quick review of how to care for my *new* car. He gave me a few rules, and said, "Tara Mae, you can do whatever you put your mind to. Remember to use your head and only depend on God."

He passed a few days after my birthday in 2014. My granny preceded him in death in 2010.

"Bossy" is something I was always called throughout life, whether in school, within my family, community, you name it. If you look up the word *bossy,* some may say it has a negative connotation. Well, being who I am, I always turn water into wine with my optimistic attitude! By definition, *bossy* means fond of giving people orders, taking charge, domineering. Yeah, you catch my drift. LOL! Well, I flipped that into queen bee, alpha female, leader, respected by all, loved by many, and ain't taking no mess!

The beautiful thing about this thang called life is you can be whoever and whatever you want to be. My mama always told me daily before getting out of the car to go into the school building, "Always do YOUR very best." And the words of my late grandpa will always ring in my ears: "That girl can do anything!" So I am doing just that...and you can too.

I appreciate your support throughout this bossy journey and I want all of my readers to get three things before beginning to read this book:

1. A pen

2. A highlighter

3. An open mind

Use this book as a personal reference guide so that when you get to the door, you will know exactly which key to use to UNLOCK it. Be true to yourself and always remember: *nothing will change if you don't.* Be well, my friends.

Key 1: The Couch

If you have goals and aspirations, chances are, you are busy! There are things you want to do, are trying to do, or have done and simply want to do again. Goals and aspirations are great, but they can bring on stress. It is what it is. Balancing everything can be a challenge, and although sometimes you can get things accomplished, other times, with life's amazing humor, things can go from 1 to 100 and FAST!

Well, that's when I head to the couch!

When I first shared with a family member that I was going to see a psychologist, she thought I was CRAY- CRAY! Lol! She told me all kinds of things:

"A shrink can't help you with your problems."

"Just pray about it."

"Only crazy people go to see psychologists."

"Black people don't believe in going to seek help from a therapist."

As crazy as it may seem, it may be taboo to even think about this as an option. But I simply looked at her response as hers, not mine. Everyone is entitled to their opinion, right?

Chile, I proceeded to make that two-hour appointment and was beyond pleased with the outcome. My psychologist made me extremely comfortable sharing my past and current issues, and her plan assisted me in becoming a healthier and better ME: mind, body, and soul. I had to be honest about what I was going through (acceptance), not allow it to consume me, yet get the help I needed.

The soft, plush gray couch was super comfy with huge oversized pillows that made me want to stay all day long. Her office was equally cozy. It had gorgeous white French doors that opened to an awaiting balcony overlooking downtown. Lavender, eucalyptus, and peppermint filled the air, making her space very welcoming. It felt like home. Once I was settled in, I knew I made the right decision for ME.

There's nothing like doing what you need to do for you. What works for you may not work for others. So if you run across naysayers, don't talk yourself out of it due to public opinion. Listen respectfully (Hey, you can learn something from anyone), and make YOUR decision for YOU.

Think about the last time you became overwhelmed and frustrated. How did you handle it? What made you select your option? If life offered do-overs, how would you handle it differently? Why?

Stop...Boss About It.

Balancing life can be challenging, yet very necessary. What can you do to continue to create balance in your life?

Stop... Boss About It.

Using Key #1: Growth and human development is necessary throughout this thing called life, and the process will happen whether we are ready or not. When I started using this key, it allowed me to learn things about myself that I would not have known otherwise.

That couch taught me that it is okay to need help and reach out for it from someone who is trained to assist. Finding a psychologist to meet my needs was easier than I thought. The hard part was making the initial step to seek help, but once I did, the floodgates opened. I had to accept where I was in my life at the moment (growth), make an asserted effort (contribution), and enjoy this season (contentment).

It's funny how people will try to sway you from making a decision that they may indeed need to make for themselves. LOL! "People" will keep you from living an abundant, fulfilled life because they are afraid to live a fulfilled life themselves. Never allow "people" who are scared to go after their dreams talk you out of yours. Be steadfast and know your crown is custom made. It will never fit anyone else.

Once you get over "people" and "they," you are on your way! This key will unlock so many doors, because knowing when you need help is half the battle. Seeking help is the other part. You cannot pour from an empty glass, so make sure your glass is full first! Know who you are, whose you are, what you possess, and who you can control...YOU. Change your mindset and it will change your life. Bossy is as bossy does.

WHEN YOUR MENTAL
IS AT PEACE,
YOUR LENSES
ARE CLEAR.
PICTURE
THAT...ENDLESS.
- TARA

Bossy Thoughts

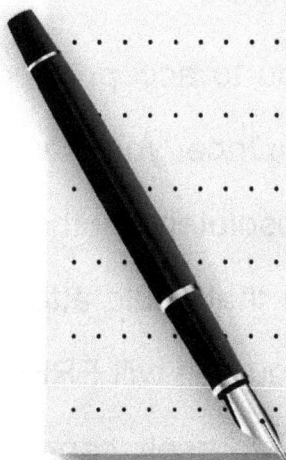

Key 2: To Thyself Be True

You may be able to fool others, but fooling yourself is a horse of a different color. Being true to thyself encompasses so much and in order to do so, you must first BE HONEST WITH YOURSELF! Who are you fooling? Live life deliberately and acknowledge your life as yours. OWN IT!

Being honest with yourself allows you to accept your TRUTHS, whatever they may be. Once you have accepted your truths, there is absolutely nothing anyone could say to you about them that could affect you in any way. Being truthful with yourself will FREE you! Why would you want to hold yourself captive anyway? You love YOU, right? If you don't, you should, and I'm sure there is plenty to love about you. Seek and ye shall FIND.

Whatever you add to your life should add value, such as spending time alone. This will definitely add value to your life because who is better to get to know than you? Some are not able to get to know others well because they don't even know themselves. Learn how to be vulnerable and straightforward with yourself, for this will allow you to develop and grow.

Listen to your thoughts and check your intentions. Be in tune with the inner you and figure out what truly makes you happy. Focus on things that bring you joy and bring out the best in you. The key word here is *focus*. Figure out what experiences will make the most positive impact and direct your attention to creating a happy space, just for you. This will allow you to put things into perspective, gain the most out of life, and reach your destiny. Live off your own energy and understand you have to rescue *yourself* first.

When you begin to love you, you will enjoy spending time alone ("Me time" is what I like to call it), with just you and your thoughts. No more drowning out the issues you have with you and surrounding yourself with numerous "besties." You will actually schedule dates with yourself - things like walks in the park, a vacation, or whatever you enjoy doing most. It'll just be you and your thoughts.

Finding balance in this complex world and time to love on you will allow you to develop awesome, fulfilling, nurturing relationships that are DESERVING OF YOU! Think about it: when was the last time you spent time with you? Put it on your calendar like all of the other important dates. Trust me, you will begin to look forward to it. :)

Some truths are hurtful, yet facing them only leads you to higher ground. What truths are most difficult for you to face? For each difficult truth, what concrete steps can you take to confront it?

Stop...Boss About It.

I discussed the importance of setting aside time for yourself or "ME time." What are some things that you could do in your "ME time"?

Stop...Boss About It.

Using Key #2: One day, I was frustrated with everyone and everything in life, including myself. I was like, "It's serious when you get tired of YOU!" However, at that point in my life, I hadn't accepted my TRUTHS. I paced my bedroom, grabbed some sticky notes and an ink pen. I wrote my truths out one at a time and placed the sticky notes on my bathroom mirror. It was full of sticky notes from issues I had not addressed, was afraid to face, or simply didn't want to accept.

I read them all aloud, screamed and cried, and promised to deal with them, one by one. I knew the road ahead would be a long one, but I was determined to accept and deal with them. As the days and months passed, I started to confront my issues, gradually yet intentionally, not rushing the process. Once I felt that the issue was accepted and fully dealt with, I removed it from my mirror and tore it to pieces, vowing never to let that issue control me ever again. The rest is history because I developed the courage to be open, honest, and sincere with myself.

I made a DECISION, took control to find my inner truth, and walked confidently in it. I created *MY* movement.

Your only focus is to remain focused. Getting, having, and keeping your stuff together is priority. With vision, you can concentrate on what's ahead and carry out the purpose within you. Don't allow your dreams to just be that...*dreams*. Acknowledge every card in your deck and *own* it. Shuffle the cards life has dealt you and play your hand. You will win some and you will lose some, but defeat is not an option. Two words: Bounce back. Remember, the only person that can beat you is YOU.

GO WHERE YOU FEEL ALIVE
AND CAN HEAR WHAT
THE UNIVERSE HAS
TO SAY TO YOU.

OPEN YOUR SOUL

AND RECEIVE WHAT'S YOURS.

- TARA

Bossy Thoughts

Key 3: Open Ya Mouth!

My granny used to always say, "A closed mouth doesn't get fed!" She was absolutely, positively correct. This adage can be applied to several situations and being "fed" has different meanings as well. I'll review a few with you because it's important that you OPEN YA MOUTH!

1. Stop saying "yes" to things you don't like or want to do. If you don't like it or don't want to do it, *you don't like it or want to do it!* It's really okay. Should everyone around you be made to feel comfortable while you're sitting there feeling uncomfortable? Negative. OPEN YA MOUTH! If you like it, cool. If you don't like it, cool. It's really that simple. Once you accept YOU... Yeah, need I say more?

2. In business, you will have to OPEN YA MOUTH! Continue to sit there like a bump on the log and see what results you get. Be assertive, network, ask questions, and work the room. There's not an app to read minds yet, so OPEN YA MOUTH! This is the only way people will know you exist.

3. When it comes to family, friends, or associates, OPEN YA MOUTH! Do not allow people to "speak" things into your life or say anything they feel like saying to you. Do not try to "save face" because of the "relationship." OPEN YA MOUTH and let them know how you feel without becoming argumentative. State your piece and let it be. Keep in mind that your decisions in life do not need the approval of others. Why seek approval of others for decisions that affect YOU? Exactly. Validation is not required when you truly approve of yourself.

Individuals who do not seek validation from others are FREE. They move about the world, dancing to the beat of their own drums, with no approval required.

Life is full of "shoulda, coulda, woulda," things that you may regret doing (or in some cases, not doing). Make a list of things that you regret. Think about how you could change those things. What can you begin doing immediately to live your life with no regrets?

Stop... Boss About It.

Do you seek validation from others? If so, why? Why might it be detrimental to seek validation from others?

Stop... Boss About It.

Using Key #3: Even as a child, I spoke up for myself and others. I did not allow people to walk over me, even if they were older. Of course, I was taught to respect my elders, but that is a two-way street.

My granny and I were all ready to go. Half of what we owned seemed to be on that bus. Lol! Granny believed in being prepared and took comfort in knowing she had what she needed for our trip. Grandpa waved goodbye as the chartered bus slowly backed out of the church's parking lot. We were headed to Atlanta to go to Six Flags Over Georgia and I was so excited, as this was my first visit to Atlanta. I was 7 years old and loved spending time with my granny. When she found out about the church trip, she knew she was taking me. She called me with the great news, and I couldn't wait to pack my bags and head to Mississippi.

After a few snacks and chats with my granny, she began humming one of her favorite songs, "Amazing Grace." Her sweet soulful hum made other people hum, and before you knew it, Granny's soothing alto-tenor voice filled the bus. It reminded you of Mahalia Jackson...that type of singing that you can feel deep down in your soul. I was in awe of how well my granny sang, often grabbing a mic and being her background singer at church. We were a duo, and no matter how many times Ms. Ryan told me I couldn't sing with my Granny, I did it anyway.

Ms. Ryan was the church's organ player. She was a mean, lil' ol' lady who never smiled. She always complained and seemed very unhappy. Well, Ms. Ryan was also on the bus.

Granny was getting to my favorite part of the song.

"I shaaaall foreeeeeever lift my eyes to Calvary...." Everyone was clapping, shouting, waving their hands, and dabbing their eyes with tissue. It truly felt like Sunday morning!

Suddenly, Ms. Ryan stood up.

"That's enough of that singing, Ida!" Ms. Ryan said gruffly. A sudden hush fell over the passengers on the bus.

"She can sing it if she wants to!" I said, with my hands on my hips. Dumbfounded, Ms. Ryan sat back down.

"Now, I bet she heard that!" Granny chuckled. She continued singing and I joined in. Soon we had the entire bus singing and shouting again!

Funny thing is, no one had ever really stood up to Ms. Ryan. Most people didn't say anything to her because she was an elder at the church, but this time, I couldn't back down. I never really understood why she was so hateful and why she loved confusion. But you know what? That was not my problem. It was hers.

After that day, Ms. Ryan was always nice to me. She would speak and ask me before church, "Are you going to sing with your granny today?" I would always respond with a respectful "Yes, ma'am." Together, my Granny and I would "tear the church up," as members of the church would say.

No matter the title or age, opening your mouth opens doors. Those who try to shush you are simply bitter and usually mad at the world. Remember that misery loves company. Singing at church opened doors of opportunity for me to sing at events, such as graduations, weddings, and family reunions. Now what if I had allowed lil' ol' Ms. Ryan to shush me? Those doors would have never opened.

Use this key and it will open doors that lead to a place where family, friends, loved ones, and people in general, will respect you because you respect YOURSELF. Never accept anything less. And guess what? If they can't, keep it pushing. Say your goodbyes and continue on your journey. You are not an *option*. Self-preservation comes first. If they can't appreciate your presence, make them appreciate your absence.

Don't be afraid to speak up, protect your space and energy, and OPEN YA MOUTH!

LIVE ON
YOUR OWN TERMS...THAT'S

WHEN LIFE
BEGINS. - TARA

Bossy Thoughts

Key 4: OKAAAAAY, I was wrong!

For the life of me, I cannot understand why people cannot admit when they are wrong!

So, let me get this straight. It's okay to make a decision to do something wrong, but it's not okay to apologize for your wrongdoing? It makes absolutely NO sense. If you can make a mistake, you should be able to apologize for it. Making excuses for wrongdoing or blaming others won't cut it.

It was cool while you were doing it, so it should be cool to say, "Hey, I was WRONG" and to apologize for it. After the apology, don't put stipulations on when the person should forgive you. Oh, and forgiving and forgetting are two *totally* different things. If they can't forgive you in the amount of time you think it should take to forgive, remove yourself, because clearly the issue lies within you. How do you do something to someone then tell him or her how long it should take to deal with it and forgive you? Chile, please!

And the worst thing you can tell a person is to get over it. Really? Obviously, people are affected in different ways when things happen to them. Be man or woman enough to apologize and let them deal with things in their own time. Actions bring on reactions. There are consequences for every decision we make in life, and we have to deal with them. It's REALLY OKAY to admit when you are wrong.

Even if you *don't* admit it, the universe knows. Remember KARMA is undefeated.

> Let's face it. We have all been wrong. We're human. Write about a time when you were reluctant to admit that you were wrong. Why do you think apologizing was so difficult?

Stop...Boss About It.

In your opinion, does admitting wrongdoing have anything to do with ego? Why or why not?

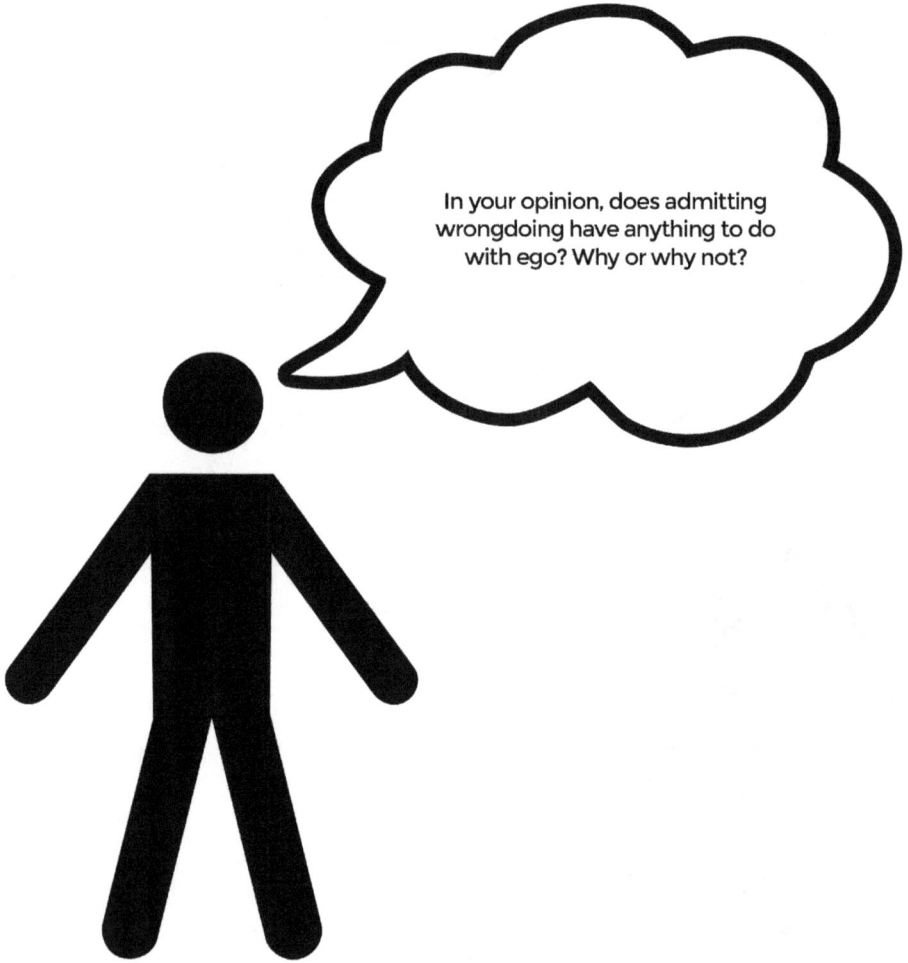

Stop... Boss About It.

Using Key #4: I have lived life long enough to know the importance of an apology…and it goes a long way. As life progresses, I always recall a lesson well learned at the tender age of nine.

When I was in fourth grade, I met and made friends with a foreign exchange student from Beijing, China named Sheri. We took swimming lessons together. One day while preparing for swim class in the girls' locker room, another student, Hannah, pushed Sheri to the ground. Hannah was certainly a bully.

Before I knew it, they were in each other's faces and our swimming coach, Miss Stacy, came running in the locker room.

"What's going on?" she yelled frantically.

"Oh, nothing!" Hannah said quickly, as if she was hiding something.

"Hannah, are you being honest with me?" Miss Stacy asked sternly.

Before Hannah could answer, Sheri and I shouted, "Nooooo!!!" in our innocent, yet matter-of-fact, nine year-old voices.

Tears begin to swell in Hannah's eyes and she sobbed for what seemed like a lifetime. She told Miss Stacy the truth about pushing Sheri to the ground.

"Well, Hannah," Miss Stacy said, "I think you owe Sheri an apology because you were wrong for pushing her. Do I need to remind you of the rules?"

"No, ma'aaaaam!" Hannah sang.

"Well, let me hear it! Apologize to Sheri, and now!" Miss Stacy demanded.

"I a-p-o-l-o-g-i-z-e!" Hannah said, slowly and nonchalantly. She twirled around and that was it.

Off to the pool we went, as Hannah stuck her tongue out at us.

I learned something that has stayed with me ever since that day. First of all, the ability to sincerely apologize is almost bigger than why you're apologizing. Hannah apologized, yet she was not sincere in doing so. It was demanded of her by authority, which was the only reason why she proceeded with the apology in the first place.

In this case, Hannah was forced to apologize although she really didn't want to. While I'm sure Miss Stacy felt as if the problem was solved, it wasn't. Although her method was ineffective, Miss Stacy did what a lot of adults do: MADE the child apologize, but the child didn't mean it. The adult thinks that she's won, but the child has, in essence, lost.

It hurt Hannah in the long run because empty words and deceit became her escape after wrongdoing, creating an inability for her to restore relationships and experience authentic reconciliation. I may not have learned how to swim (LOL...that's another story), but I learned a valuable lesson early in life and one that I will never forget.

SINCE NO ONE IS PERFECT, ADMITTING A WRONG SHOULD BE A SIMPLE PROCESS. NOPE...SOMETIMES IMPOSSIBLE. - TARA

Bossy Thoughts

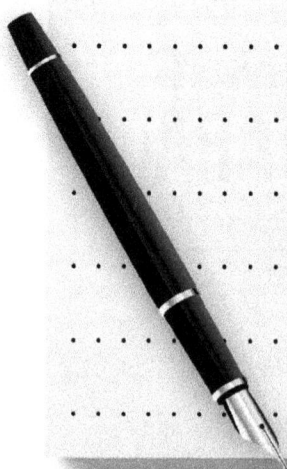

Key 5: Co-Exist: Live & Let Live

To co-exist means to be able to exist in mutual tolerance despite different ideologies or interests. This is by far one of my most rewarding abilities. Because of my ability to co-exist, I have been able to meet some of the most interesting people in the world. Building and growing life-long relationships throughout my global travels have afforded me so many opportunities for growth, whether personal or business related.

Networking is essential to business growth and potential. With a positive attitude and the ability to co-exist, doors will open that you thought may have never ever, ever existed.

You may ask, "If I've looked at my life and come to the conclusion I am currently not co-existing, what can I do to change that?" Well, I'm glad you asked! LOL!

Here are 3 things you can do to start co-existing TODAY!

1. Go somewhere you have never been, probably wanted to go, but didn't think you'd fit in. Be sure to take your OPEN mind with you and a sense of humor. Look around, without judgment. What do you see? Who is there? Why did you think you wouldn't fit in originally? Strike up a conversation with someone and let the universe work its magic. It will probably be a moment of AWAKENING! Broadening your understanding will allow you to gain new knowledge that can be applied to multiple aspects of your life. Become tolerant and start LIVING!

2. Make a list of your insecurities. We all have either had them at some point or still have them. Deal with

your insecurities, one by one. Create a game plan to change YOU instead of changing others, which is what we attempt to do when we JUDGE. It will lighten your load, and you will find inner PEACE. Living in peace is both an outward and inward process. Usually, once you accept YOU, you have no problem accepting others. Reflect on your list until your insecurities are at zero! Take a pause for the cause, breathe, discover your own light, and proceed. Your new life is waiting, but you have to give up your old one first.

3. Reflect and think about the people in your life. Do you attempt to control others with your words and actions? Those are called *control dramas*. Do your research. Control dramas are **very** interesting. Once you do your research, you will find that several people (you included) have probably tried to run your life with control dramas.

Some people who have an issue with co-existing usually have an issue with trying to control others as well. But let me ask a question. How can you attempt to control other people's lives, yet you aren't in control of your own? Chile, please! You are wasting your precious time on something that is not even your business. Focus on YOU!

Life is complicated enough. Adding the task of controlling someone else's life only further complicates the situation. Sweep around your own front door. I'm more than positive you will find enough to keep you occupied.

I spent time researching control dramas during my junior and senior years in high school and I learned valuable information that has really assisted me throughout life. Did you know control dramas existed? Why do you think people become controlling? Why might some people allow themselves to become victims of control dramas?

Stop...Boss About It.

Changing your mindset can change your life. What are you willing to change to create a better life for yourself?

Stop...Boss About It.

Using Key #5: Growing up, I was very active in school and participated in several extracurricular activities. I played the piano, played the trumpet in the school band, sang in the church and school choirs, was active in the Girl Scouts, the National Junior and Senior Honor Societies, Student Government Association, Beta Club, Mu Alpha Theta (the math honor society), and the list goes on. It was imperative to co-exist with this busy schedule, because I encountered I all types of people, learned about different cultures, religions, traditions, values, morals, music, food, you name it. My mama was a huge proponent of exposing me to everything life had to offer and always made sure I had the best of everything, especially education.

Because of my upbringing, I was able to carry what I learned from home throughout my life, accepting people as they are. The ability to tolerate people, no matter what, has allowed me to encounter endless opportunities for personal and professional growth. Being able to co-exist in a colorful world continues to allow me to meet the greats of the world and establish life-long relationships.

I remember my first day as a middle school teacher. I was calling the roll when a student knocked on the door. I opened it and warmly welcomed the young man to my classroom.

"Are you Mrs. Seals?" he asked nervously.

"Yes, sir. Are you enrolled in my class?"

He hesitated. "Yes, but I am afraid to come in."

"Why?" I asked.

"Because the other kids will make fun of me. They've been making fun of me all day in all my other classes."

By this time he was on the verge of tears.

It was fourth period and I guess he had taken all he could take.

"Gimme just a moment, sir." I stepped back into my classroom. "Ladies and gentlemen, go ahead and get started on your 'Who Am I?' assessment. I'd like to hear a few really good responses when I return."

When I stepped back into the hallway, the young man explained to me that he was a homosexual male and the students were picking on him because he carried a purse, wore artificial nails and lashes, and was feminine. I listened attentively as he went on to tell me about his day up until this point. Trust me when I say that he'd had enough.

After a few minutes of allowing him to vent and get everything off his chest, I asked him a question that shifted the entire vibe of the conversation.

"Gregory, do *you* have a problem with you?"

He paused for a moment.

"Uh, no, I like myself very much. It's these kids. They're the ones with the problem!" he said assertively.

"Well, there you have it. They have the problem, not you!" I gave him a reassuring smile. "Look, you won't have that issue in my class. Our goal in here is to take care of business. My motto is, 'If you're not here for business, you have no business here!' Do you mind if I talk to the class about how you've been treated and how you felt?"

His eyes grew big. "Would you really do that?"

"Of course!" I replied.

Gregory smiled and walked into my classroom with a newfound sense of confidence. We took a break from my planned lesson and used Gregory's first day as a teachable moment and had a great discussion about accepting people for who they are. I also urged my students not to limit their mind to only what they deem as "acceptable."

From that point on, Gregory excelled academically. He was a bright student with aspirations to become a registered nurse. Guess what? He is living the life he worked so hard for. Because of his tenacity, he became the first person in his family to graduate from college and is currently a RN. None of this would have been possible if he dwelt in his insecurities and allowed the opinions of others to shape who he was.

Co-existence is the epitome of living a full life with no regrets. Try it--you just may like it. Accepting others as they come will open doors.

Remember to live life *in* and *on* purpose!

HOW YOU ACCEPT OTHERS SHOWS HOW YOU ACCEPT YOURSELF.

ACTIONS MY FRIENDS.

- TARA

Bossy Thoughts

The Reflect

Life is about experiences, not appearances. Andddddd it's short, so live it YOUR way, unapologetically. You truly have the power to choose; you just have to make a choice and guess what? Making a choice *can* be effortless. We do it every day, even with simple things, like deciding what's for dinner. Sometimes we complicate life when it doesn't have to be complicated at all! LOL!!

Now, let me be clear--the decision you make could be the best one, or the worst one. But the fact is that YOU are the one who makes the choice. Confront your fears instead of allowing them to control you. That's a step in the right direction. Remember, you don't have to be great to start, but you have to start to be great.

If things don't turn out the way you expect, reshuffle your cards and choose again, but now play your hand using the new knowledge you learned from the last decision you made. It's never a loss, but a lesson.

I have already used the keys, so I know that they work. I hope by sharing these keys with you, you'll be able to maximize your time and live your best, *bossy* life. Hey, saving time is essential when living bossy. I'll never waste your time or mine.

It is always my goal to give back to others as others have given to me. We must pass the baton and teach every soul who is willing to listen and gain knowledge. It's up to us to receive it, apply it, and achieve it. Think of it this way: a short term investment for a lifetime of opportunity.

I've left 5 keys under the doormat with your name on each one. All you have to do is make a choice to reach for them, insert the keys in the locks and turn them to the open the doors.

Don't forget to share with others and always remember:

Bossy is as bossy does.

Until next time,

Tara

www.ingramcontent.com/pod-product-compliance
Lightning Source LLC
Chambersburg PA
CBHW070639150426
42811CB00050B/399